THE PRAYING ATHLETE™

PHOTOGRAPHY

QUOTE BOOK - VOL 1

Robert B. Walker

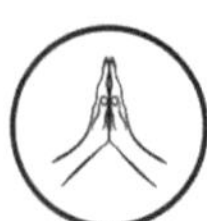

The Praying Athlete Photography Quote Book Volume 1

Published by The Core Media Group, Inc., P.O. Box 2037, Indian Trail, NC 28079.

Quotes written by Robert B. Walker. Photography by Robert B. Walker. Cover and interior design by Ashlyn Helms.

Printed in the United States of America.

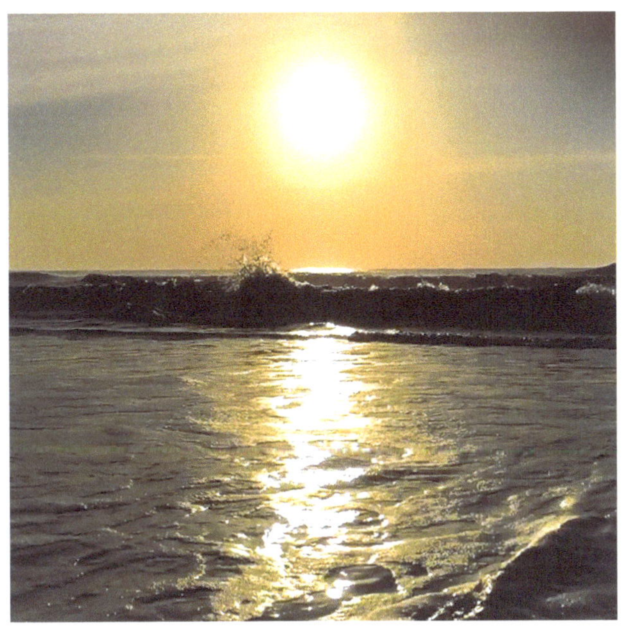

"The waves of life will keep coming. Even through all the storms, never stop believing that tomorrow can be better than today!"

"Sometimes in life, we may drift away from what we know is right. The drift wood symbolizes each of us—we have all been here. The negativity of life comes at us hard. We can allow it to make us feel like we are all washed up, because of our mistakes or negative thoughts, but that is not TRUTH! The footprint symbolizes God coming to our rescue. We only see one set of footprints in the photo as He carries us and sets our ways straight. The rainbow symbolizes the hope we have in God, and the good He wants for each of us. Never doubt God is near in everything. Keep pressing on during the journey."

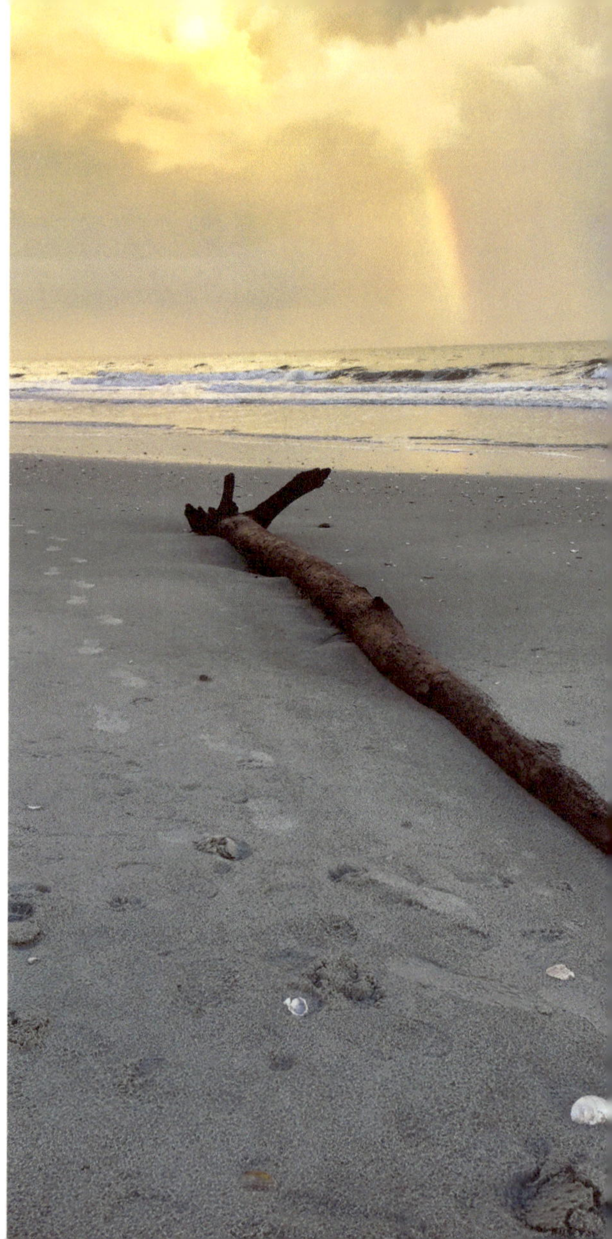

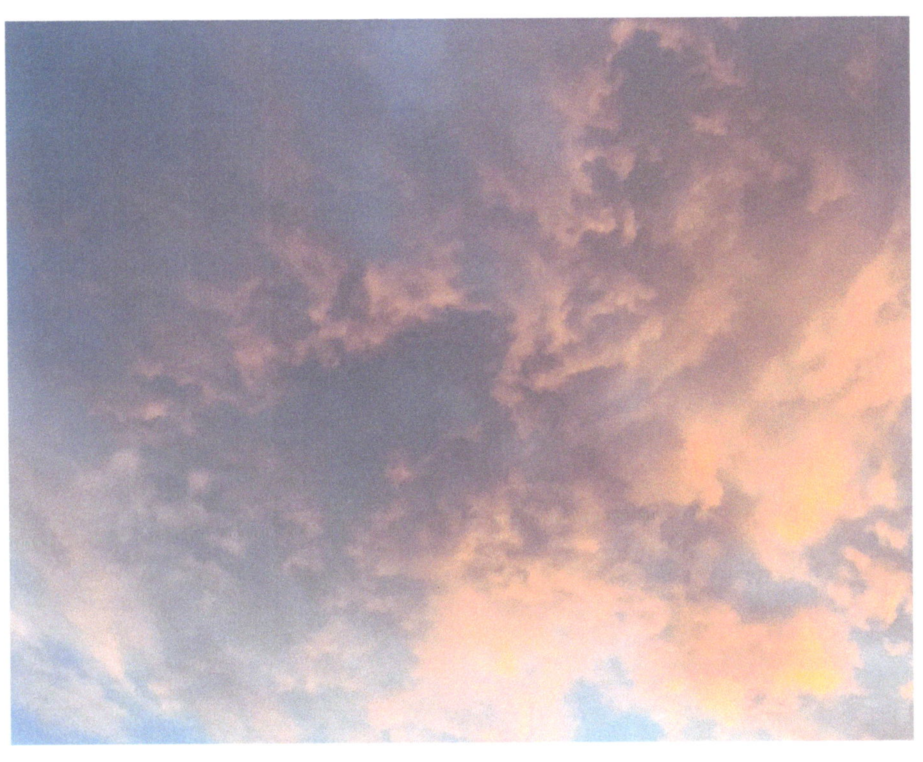

"The voice of calculation in life can suppress and stress us. The voice of faith will free and relieve us."

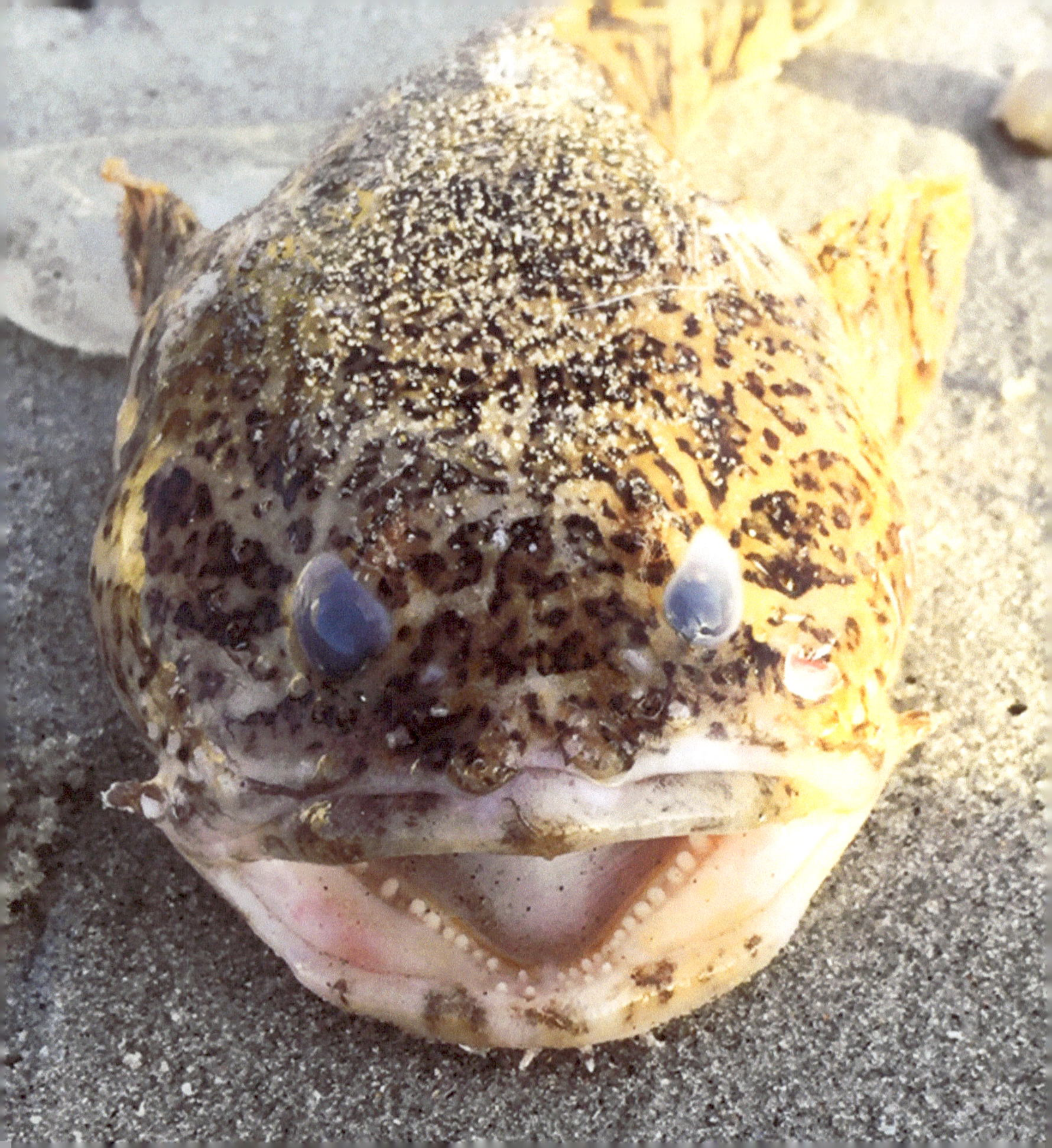

"Start every day with a smile no matter your circumstances."

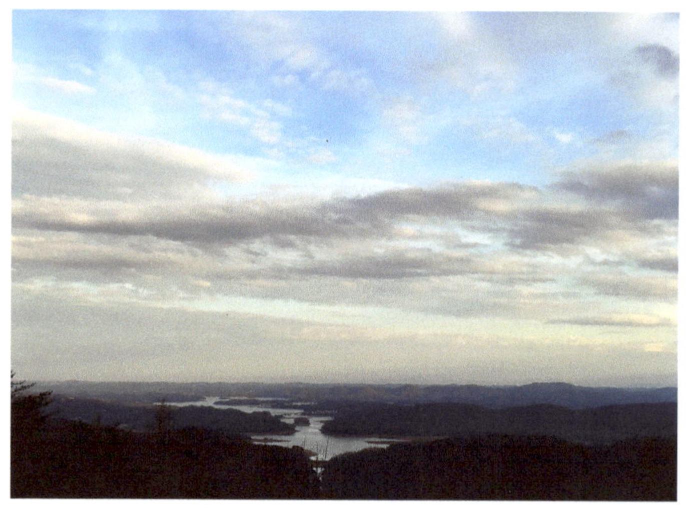

"It could be a long journey to the water you need in life, but keep your eyes focused on your goals and what you want and you will soon arrive to the area you are thirsty for."

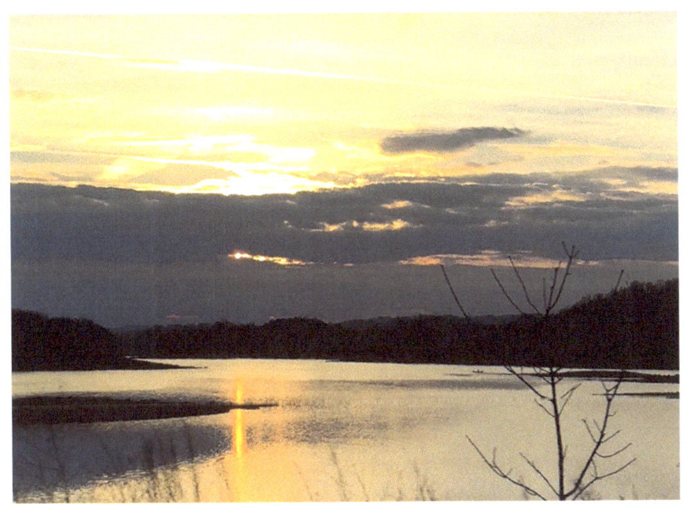

"There is a misconception that age can sometimes keep people apart and keep them from achieving and pursuing, but it is the heart that will keep you a part of each other. Let no one tell you how to manage your heart, that is yours."

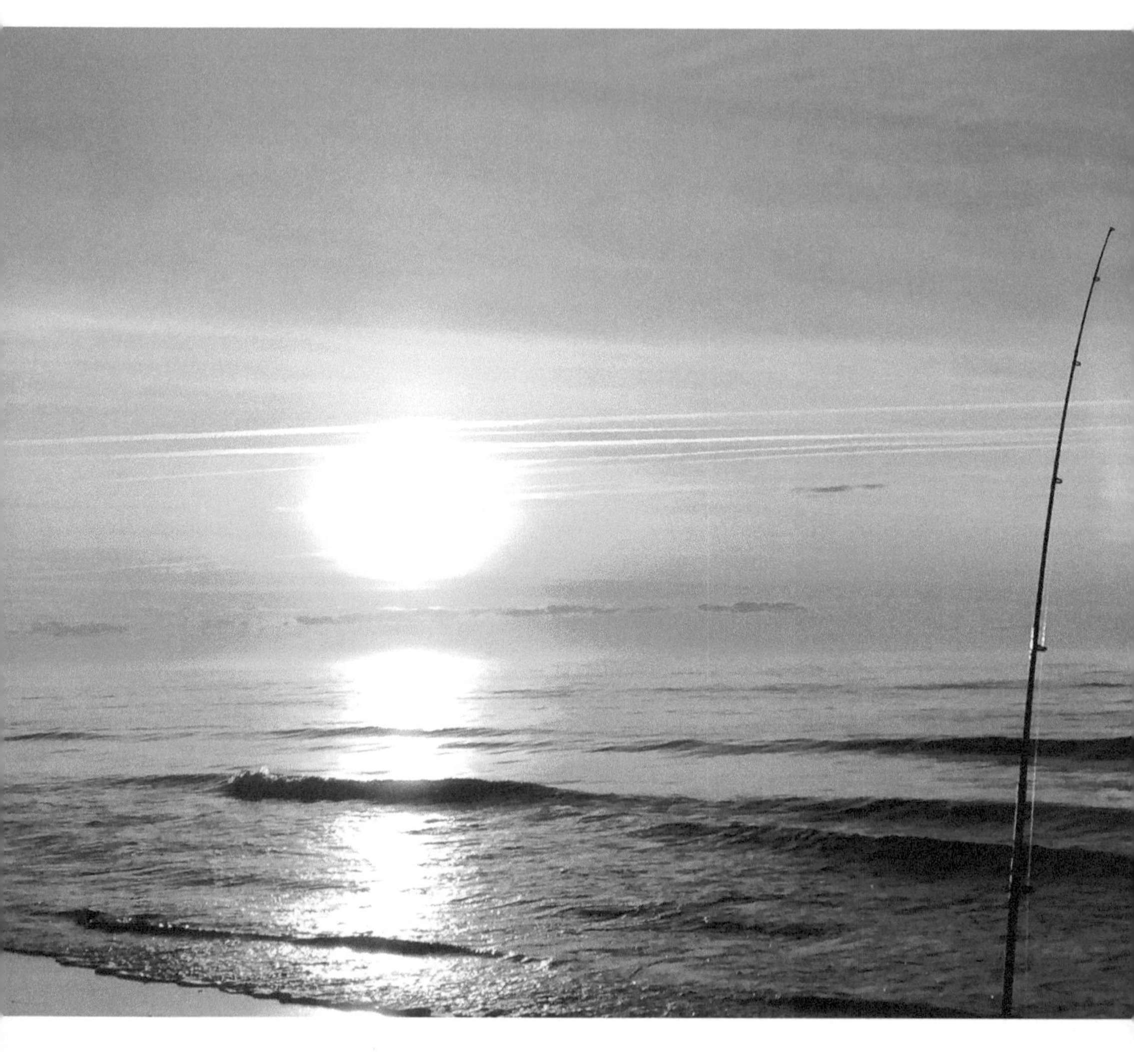

"Happiness in life comes to those that try to find it. Cast a line today—you may catch your dream. If not, keep casting because it is out there."

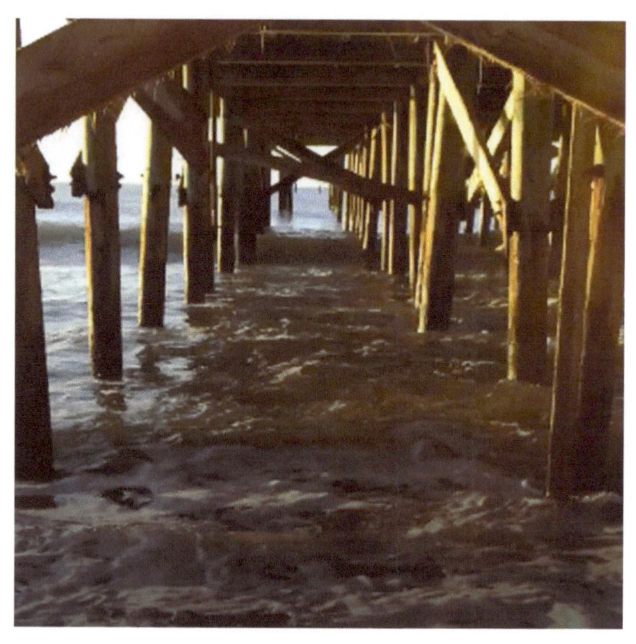

"Plant your roots deep to withstand the pressures and pounding of life."

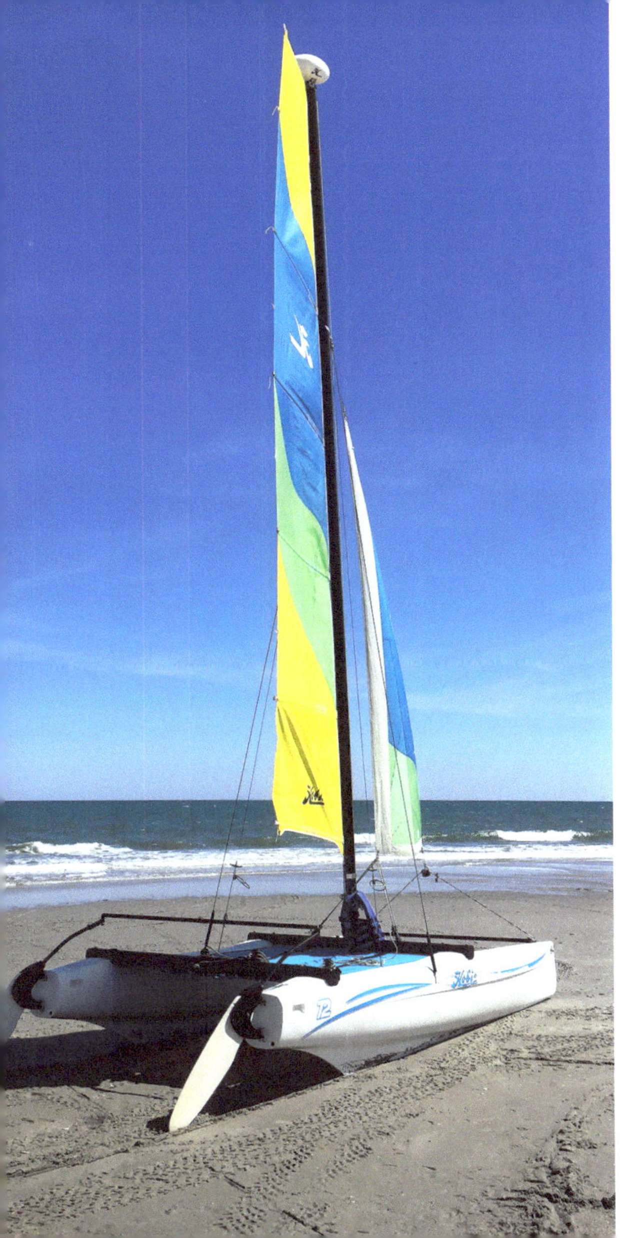

"You cannot sail away to
your destination if you never
take any risk."

"Every day is a fresh start for your new adventures and journeys in life. I often wonder if that is why the birds sing so loud as the sun begins to rise. Maybe they are just happy to have survived the night. May we all have song in our hearts as we embrace each new day that we are Blessed to receive."

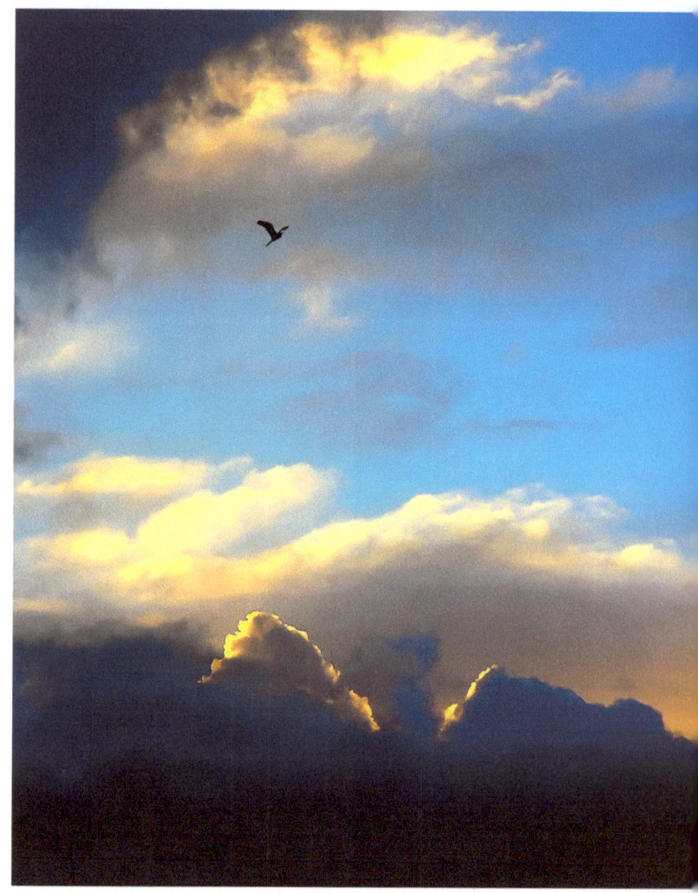

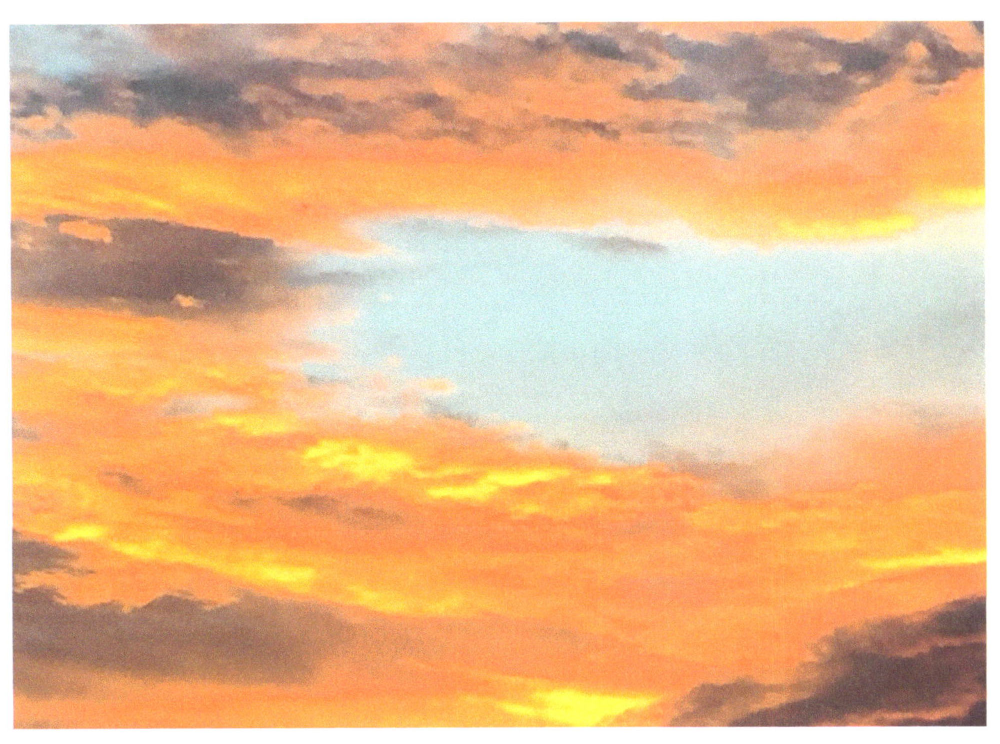

"Park your negativity, and fuel up on the right fuel to reach your dreams!"

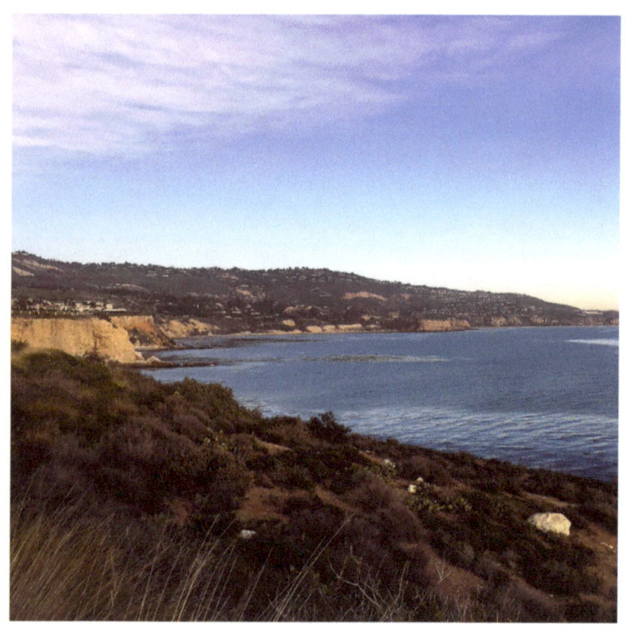

"The success of each day is built on the little moments of focus, desire, preparation, determination, wisdom, drive, and energy toward your daily goal."

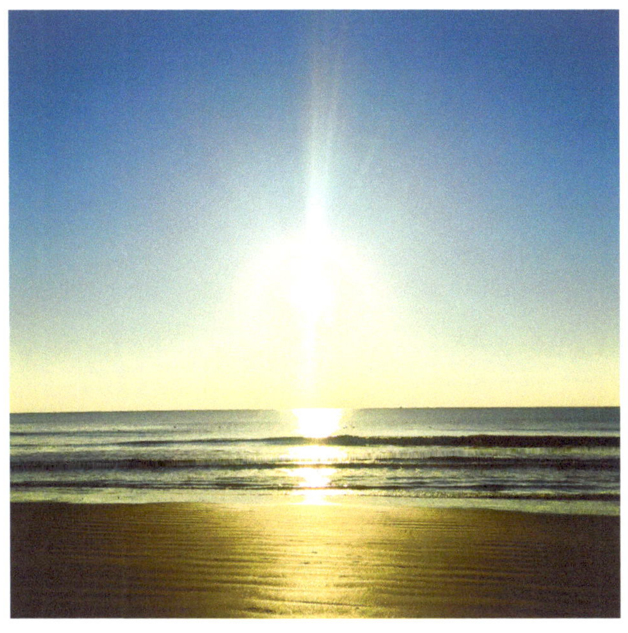

"Life can fly by. Take time to see the sun rise with those you love."

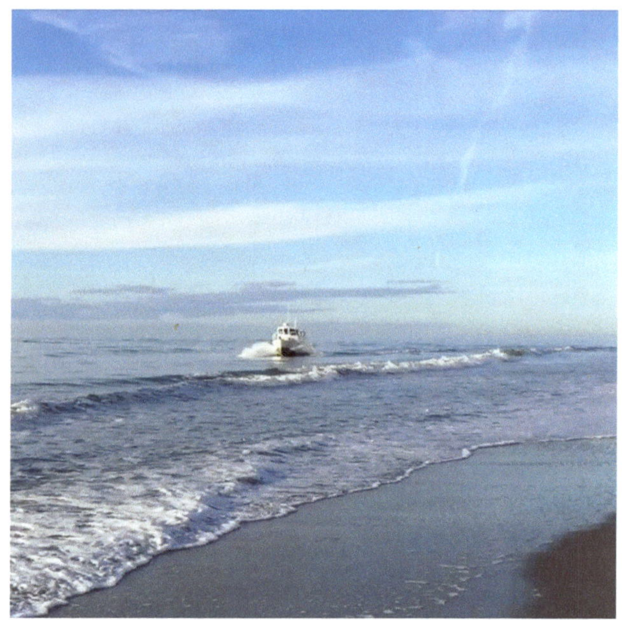

"Staying close to the shoreline will never allow you to catch the big dreams of life. It is risky, the waters will be deep and the storms will be intense, but you will survive, thrive and live out your dreams."

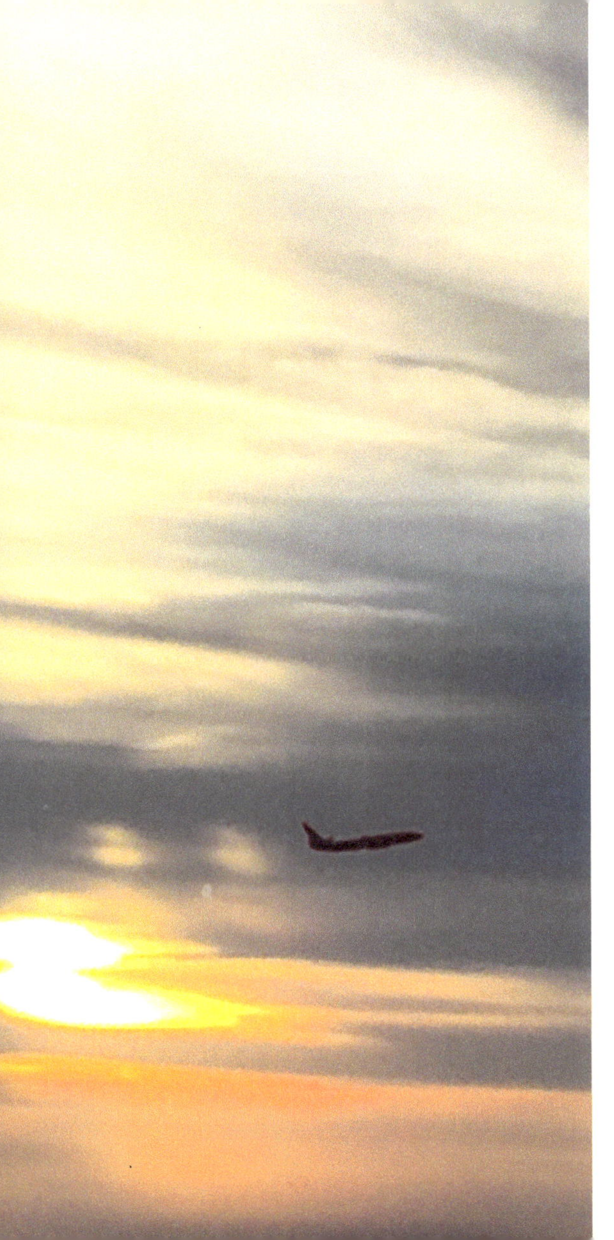

"Always look closely, and you will see God flying in reinforcements to help you overcome life challenges."

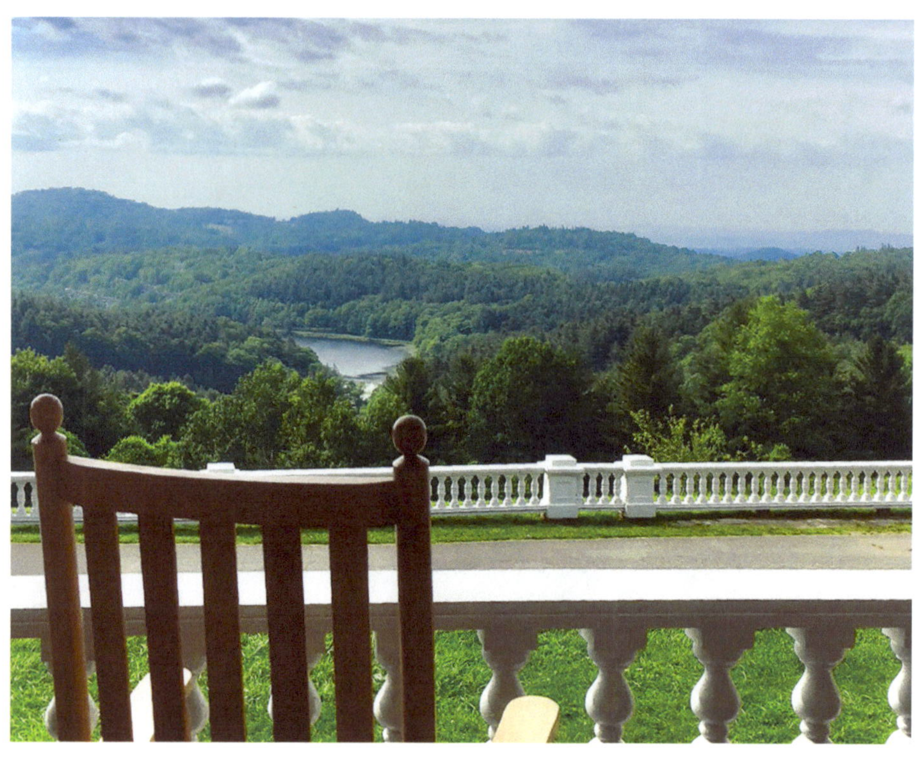

"Prepare today and your time will come! Seize and capture every moment and every second of time. Redeem daily the plans that are in your heart. Work to push all the negative thoughts away, for they can ground you from the desires in your mind and heart. Soon you will fill this seat and reflect on all the goodness God has put into your life. You will win this battle because you have intensity and the heart of a champion. Now Believe it, Claim it, Do it!"

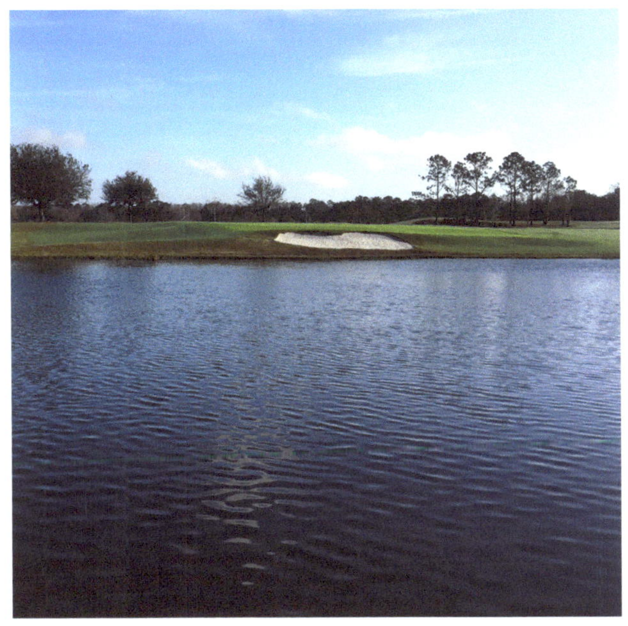

"During our life, we will fall into traps and be challenged. The trap is never as big as we make it out to be. Keep chipping away and you will soon overcome whatever the obstacles may be. The green grass is so close. Keep going!"

"When you think the race is finished, it is just beginning. One victory does not mean the race of life is completed. Keep pushing!"

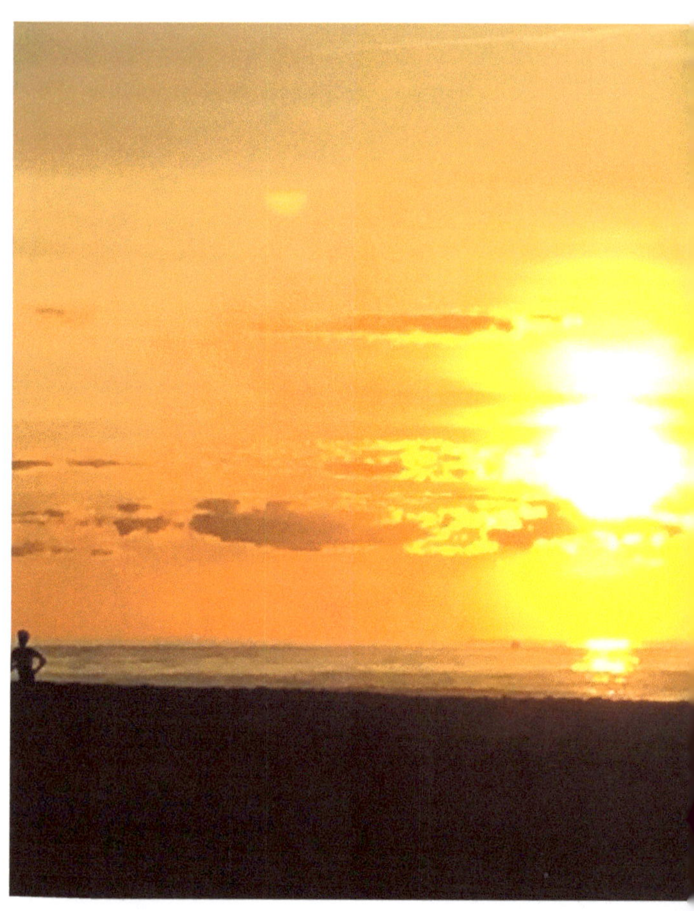

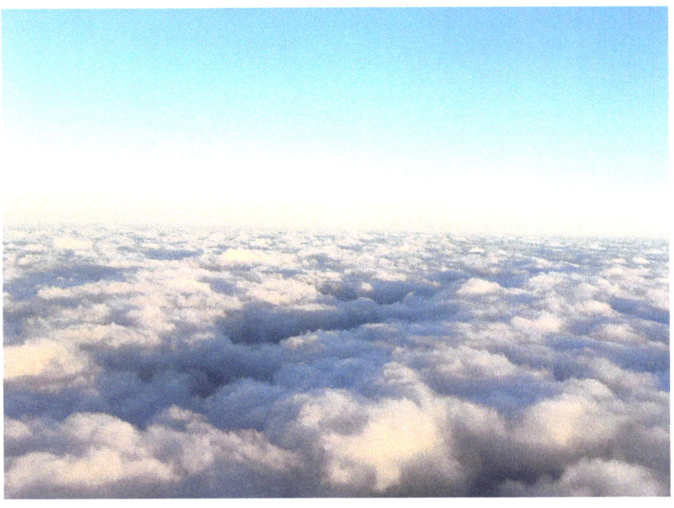

"When you are EFFICIENT and EFFECTIVE, you will be EMPOWERED to overachieve and overcome."

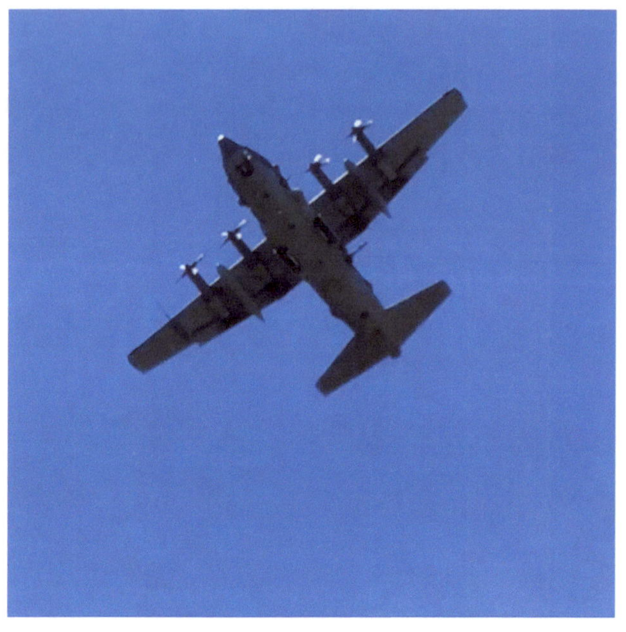

"What kind of cargo or baggage are you carrying? Sometimes you have to drop the baggage and cargo to reach the peak of your success."

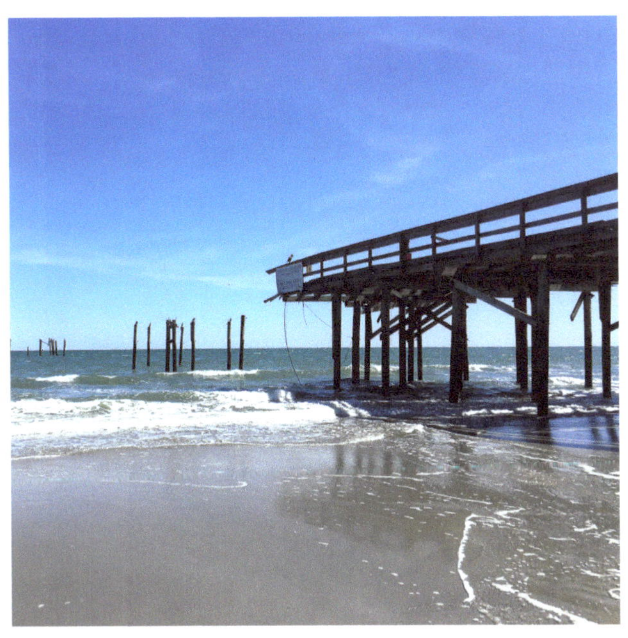

"The storms of life will try and rip you apart. The last time I checked, you were still standing. It is time to build a stronger foundation so you will be ready for the next storm and sustain the strong tides."

"Today may be challenging and many days will be distracting. However, maintain a continuous flow to the goals you have set."

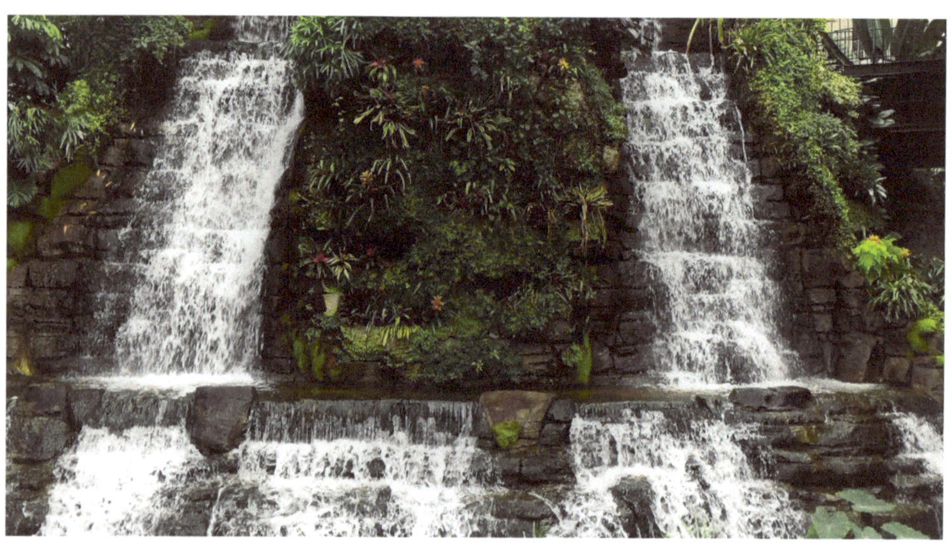

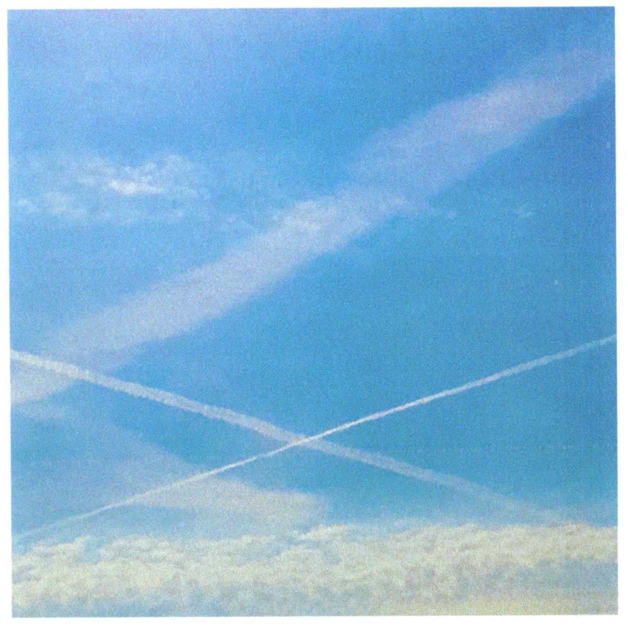

"What do you need to X out of your life
to reach your sky high potential?"

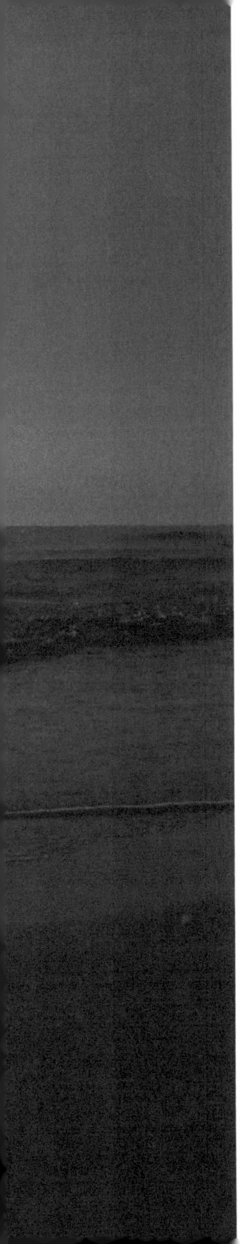

"The pain of heartbreak can be intense and misunderstood. However, pain is actually the first step to healing. We cannot heal if we never embrace the pain and hurt. Jesus experienced the greatest hurt and His healing was marvelous. His healing brought a new Life and a new Body. So, as much as it hurts, know it is better to go through the pain than to live in the pain and hurt for an entire life. The healing may seem long, but in the scope of life it is very short. So remember, the pain is actually healing masked."

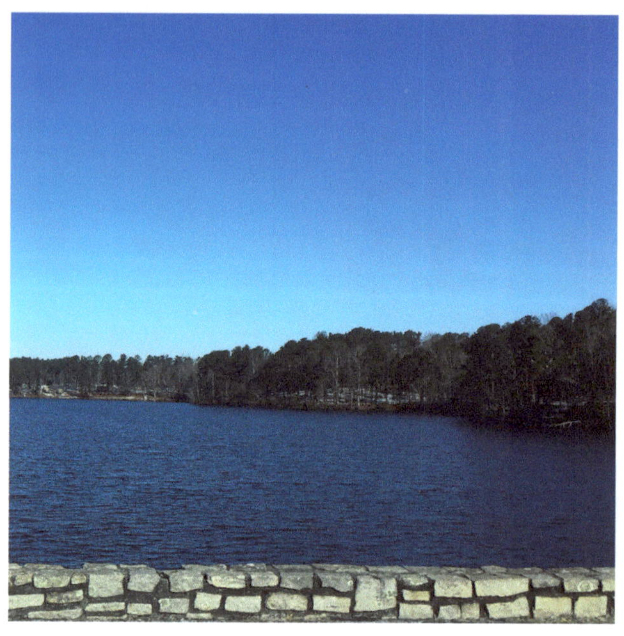

"Man gives a position, but God defines and gives you purpose in life. Once you engage your purpose, God will give you a position to elevate and empower you beyond what you ever thought possible."

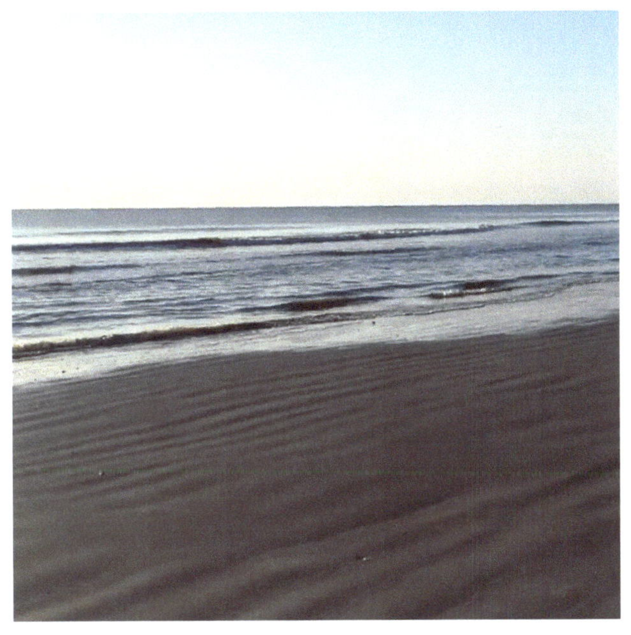

"We are always in motion! The ocean moves everyday. The waves come to the shoreline 24/7. There is purpose in the ocean's motion. Does your motion have purpose? If so, what is the purpose? Make your motion count everyday just like the ocean!"

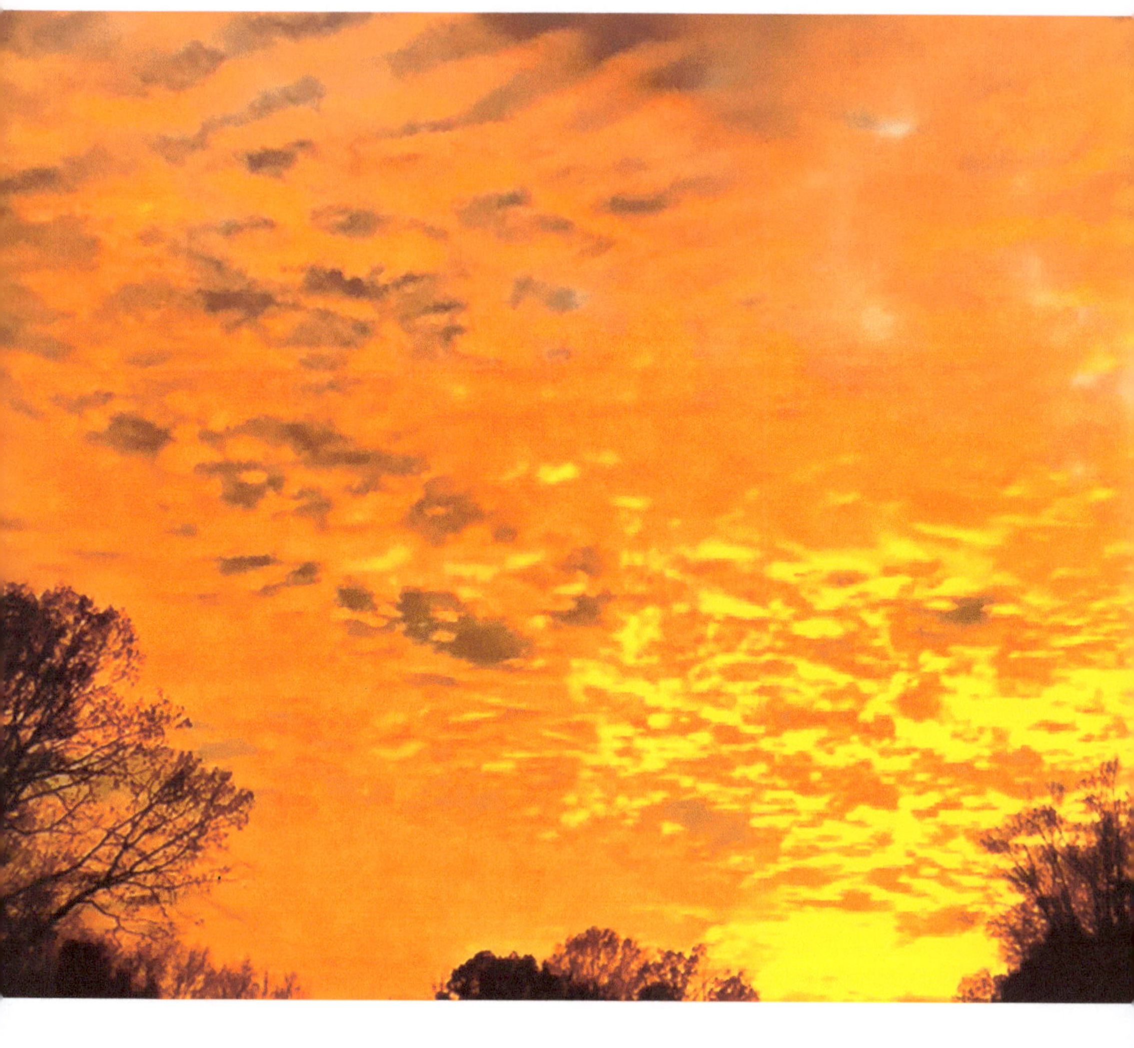

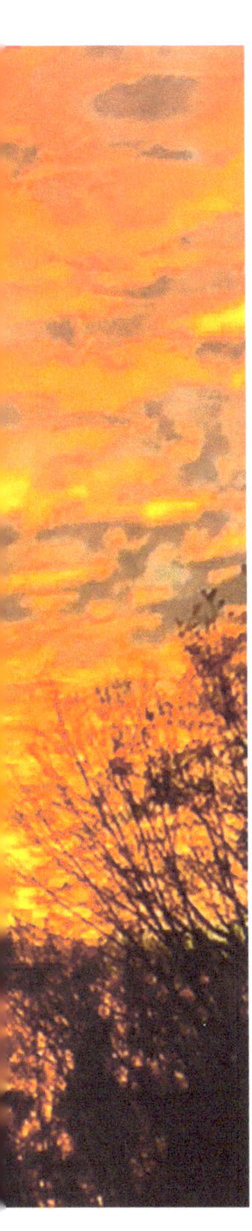

"Work your PURPOSE, reach your POTENTIAL."

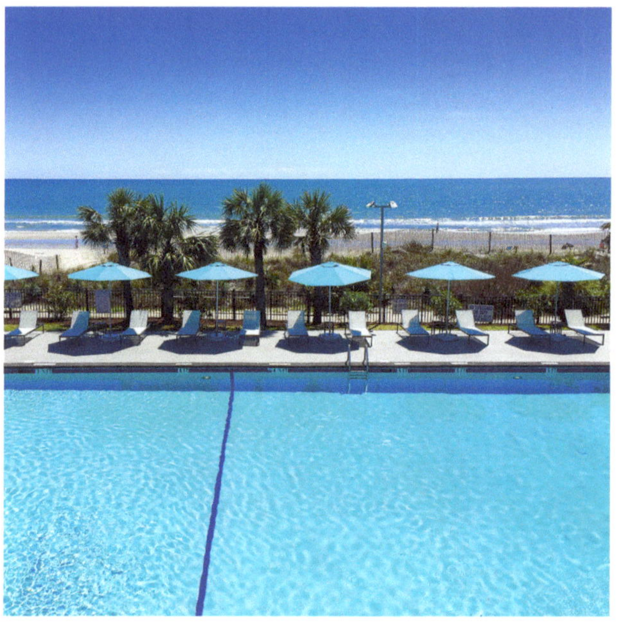

"To get here will take work and focus. But once here, know that this is temporary and only happened because you were focused and put in the work."

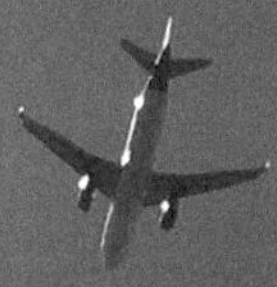

"Everyday do something to TAKE OFF and make your dreams happen. If you do nothing, you will stay grounded with nothing but time passing you by. TAKE OFF today."

"What is your view of life? This picture is outstanding, so many fun things to be a part of. However, remember the work it took to create this view—so many people, the right equipment, the planning, the patience and on and on. If you have a view for your life, it will and can happen. It will require a tremendous amount of effort on your part and those around you. Dream It, Create It, Plan for It, Go get It, View It!"

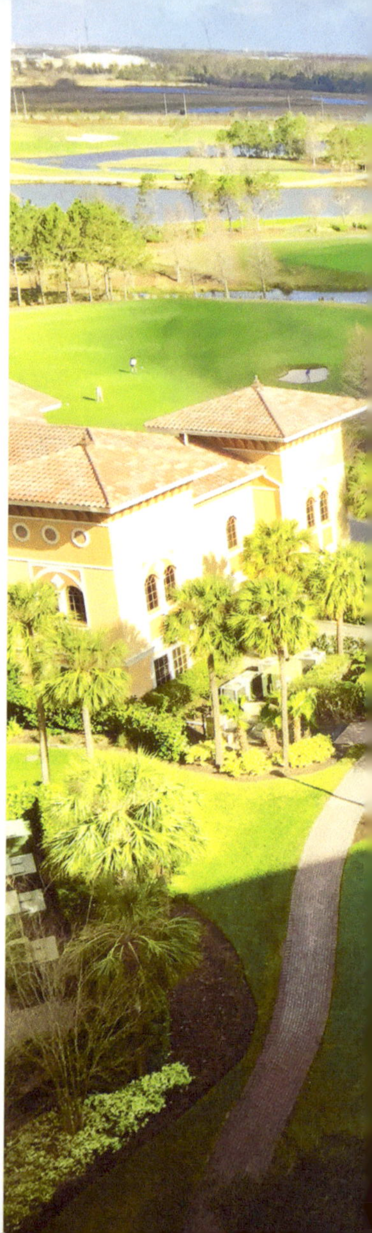

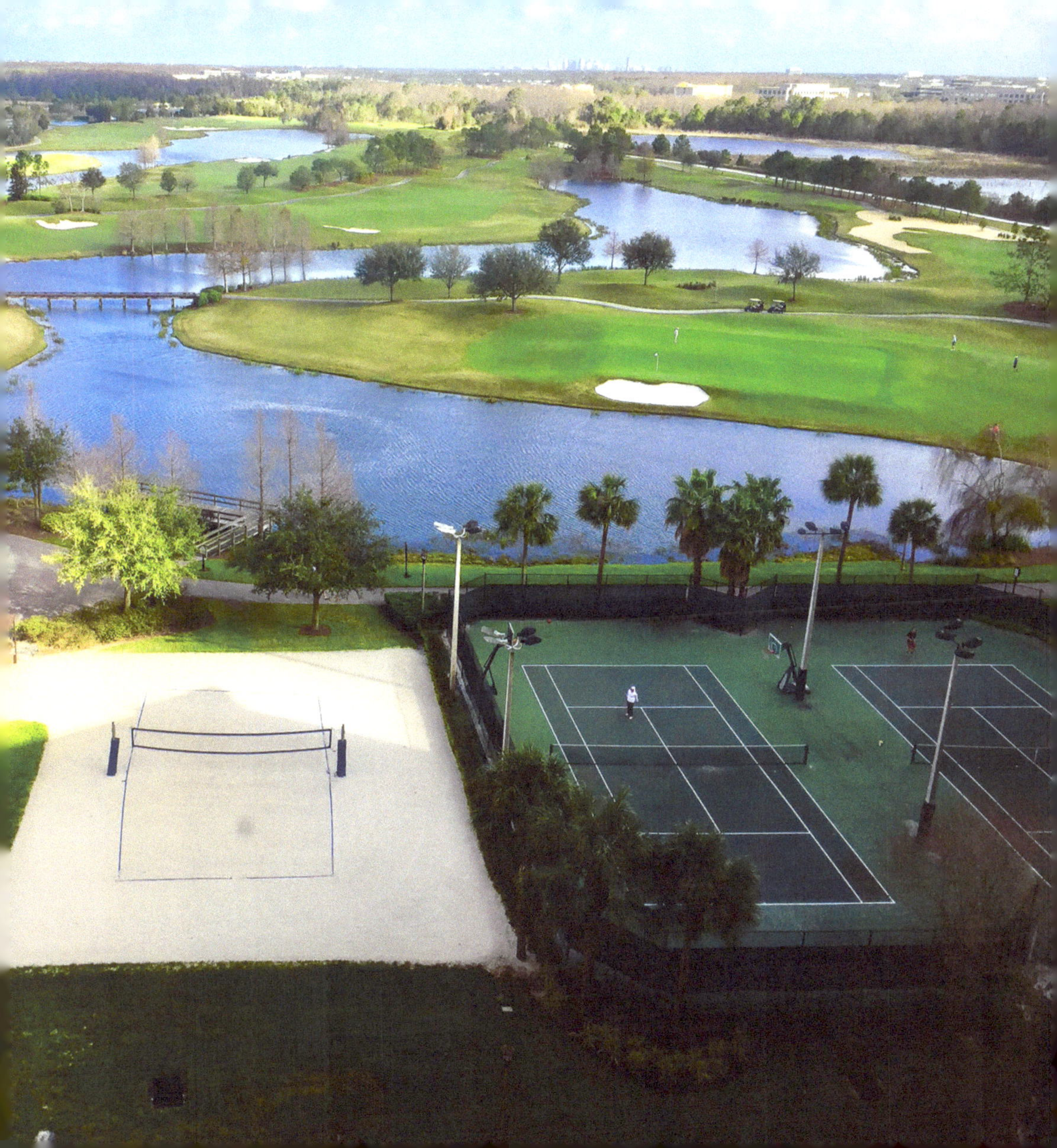

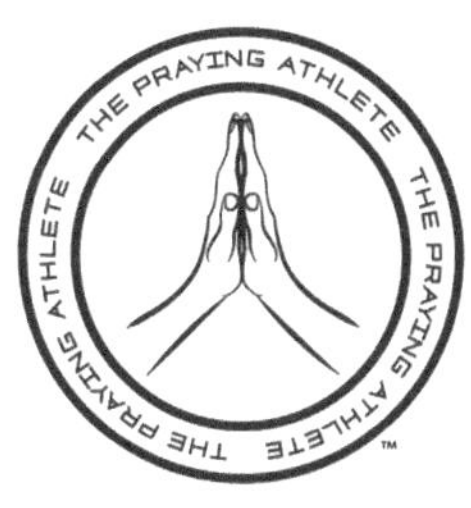

ABOUT TPA

The Praying Athlete is a movement that creates an organic culture of prayer through an uplifting community and authentic conversation.

For more information, visit our website **www.theprayingathlete.com**.

Follow us on social media.

 **@ThePrayingAthlete**

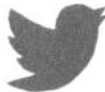 **@Praying_Athlete**

 **@ThePrayingAthlete**

CHECK OUT OUR

THE PRAYING ATHLETE™

QUOTE BOOK SERIES

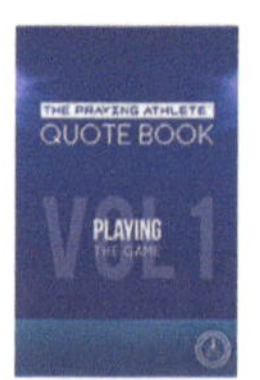

Our first volume of *The Praying Athlete Quote Book* addresses the topic of playing the game. Quotes and thoughts from Robert B. Walker, paired with Scripture from God's Word, allow readers to get a good idea about what playing a good game looks like.

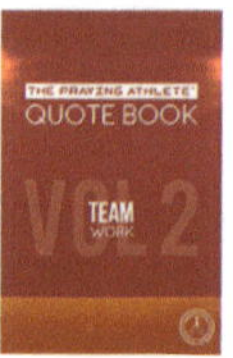

Our second volume of *The Praying Athlete Quote Book* addresses the topic of teamwork. Quotes and thoughts from Robert B. Walker, paired with Scripture from God's Word, allow readers to understand what it means to be a good teammate and surround yourself with people who lift you up.

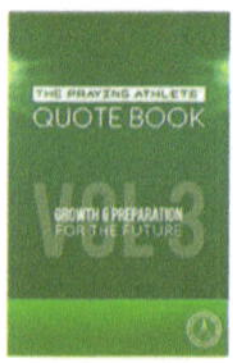

Our third volume of *The Praying Athlete Quote Book* addresses the topic of growth & preparation for the future. Quotes and thoughts from Robert B. Walker, paired with Scripture from God's Word, allow readers to know that even though the future is uncertain, there is a plan and purpose for everyone.

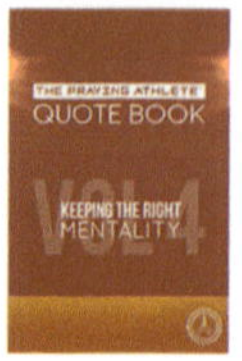

Our fourth volume of *The Praying Athlete Quote Book* addresses the topic of keeping the right mentality. Quotes and thoughts from Robert B. Walker allow readers to understand how staying in the right mindset can improve overall performance.

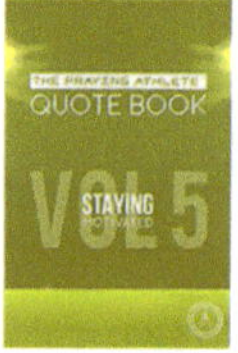

Our fifth volume of *The Praying Athlete Quote Book* addresses the topic of staying motivated. Quotes and thoughts from Robert B. Walker allow readers to become motivated to accomplish their goals, even when they feel they are not up to the task.

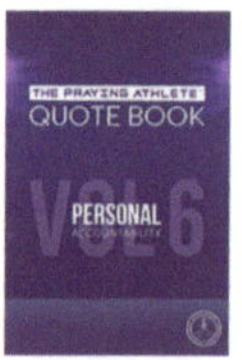

Our sixth volume of *The Praying Athlete Quote Book* addresses the topic of personal accountability. Quotes and thoughts from Robert B. Walker allow readers to think about how they can better themselves. Whether its ending a bad habit or saying no to anything that may hurt themselves or others, staying accountable will benefit one's character and performance.

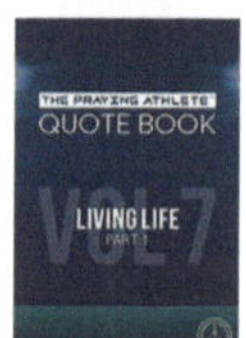

Our seventh volume of *The Praying Athlete Quote Book* addresses the topic of living life. This volume is the first part in a two part living life series. Quotes and thoughts from Robert B. Walker give readers a better understanding of how to live life to the fullest.

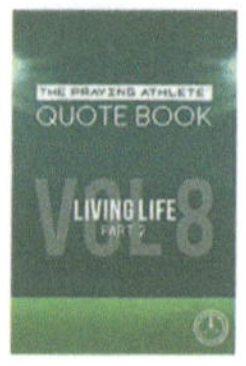

Our eighth volume of *The Praying Athlete Quote Book* addresses the topic of living life. This volume is the second part in a two part living life series. Quotes and thoughts from Robert B. Walker give readers a better understanding of how to live life to the fullest.

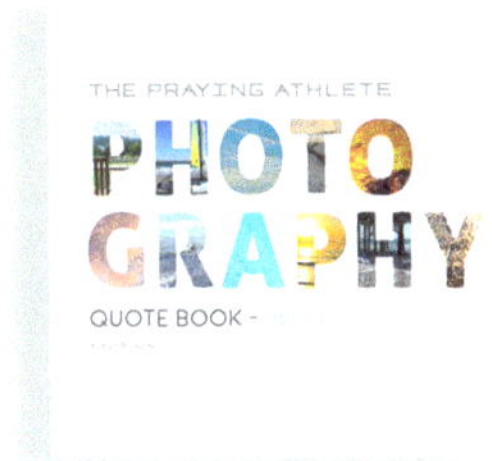

VOL. 1

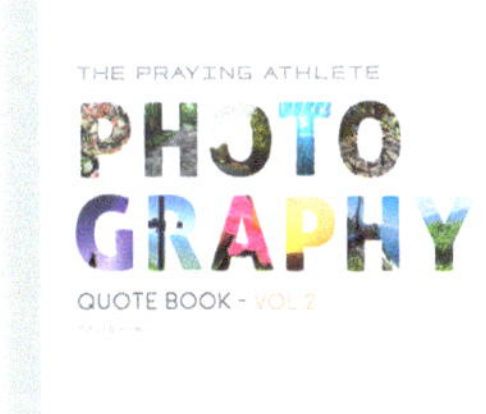

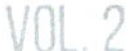

VOL. 2

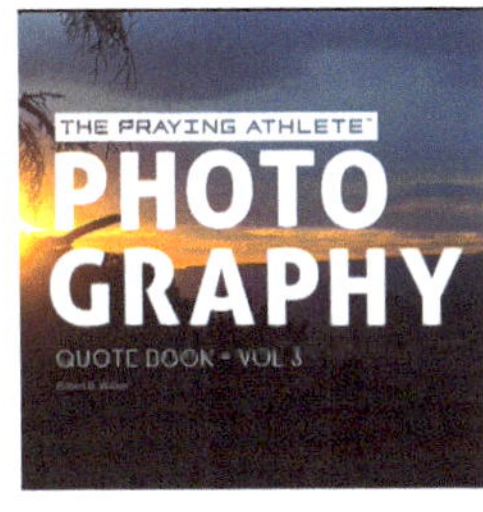

VOL. 3

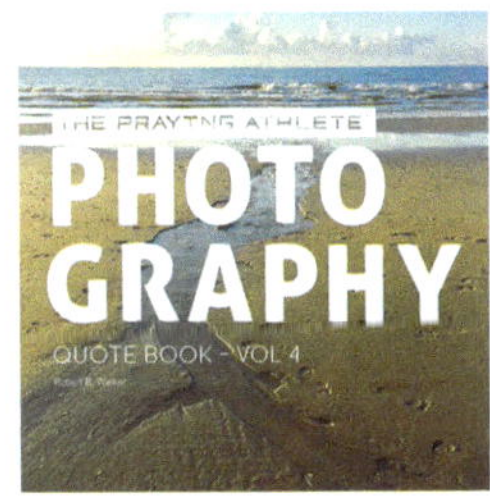

VOL. 4

The Praying Athlete Photography Quote Books celebrate God's glory and magnificence through His creation. They contain photos taken by Robert B. Walker, paired with his words of wisdom, motivation, and inspiration.

www.ingramcontent.com/pod-product-compliance
Lightning Source LLC
LaVergne TN
LVHW070156110826
845147LV00002B/419

* 9 7 8 1 9 5 0 4 6 5 1 3 2 *